10655232

LEON

Breakfast & Brunch

NATURALLY FAST RECIPES

LEON

Breakfast & Brunch

NATURALLY FAST RECIPES

By Henry Dimbleby, Kay Plunkett-Hogge, Claire Ptak & John Vincent

PHOTOGRAPHY BY GEORGIA GLYNN SMITH · DESIGN BY ANITA MANGAN

conran
OCTOPUS

Contents

Introduction

Hubris is said to cause the collapse of empires. There's danger in getting too big for one's boots. In feeling invincible. More important than others. So it is with some hesitancy that we confirm the rumour that breakfast probably is the MOST IMPORTANT MEAL OF THE DAY. It deserves a rosette. Or at least a sash. Or a badge it can sew on to its tracksuit.

And it's true: our own lives, serving people who eat with us at Leon, our research, and our work in school food, have all taught us the power of a good breakfast. It's why we focus so much effort on our porridges (try Porridge and add a banana or dark chocolate topper, see page 10), and why we created the Posh Poached Eggs in a Cup made with chorizo and truffled cheese (see page 26). And it's why we've created a range of breakfast muffins made with spelt, a good alternative to modern wheat. And it's why we bring you this little book.

Now, let's keep things positive. Let's not preach that 'commercial' cereals are mostly wheat and sugar, spiking blood sugar in a not-so-wonderful way. Let's instead explore and enjoy all of the ways we can release ourselves from the tyranny of that rectangular box.

We know you have a lot on. So we've kept these recipes simple. But you can't make things you don't have in your house. (Is that a bit obvious?). So a little thinking ahead will help with your mission.

Please share with us what ideas and approaches work well for you. For example, we find it good to combine good fats with good carbs; we have walnuts or seeds with our porridge. And when making pancakes, we make them with buckwheat, which is naturally free from gluten.

Most of all, we hope you find these recipes a wonderful way of enjoying your breakfasts, your morning and your life. We like them. Happy cooking.

Henry & John

GRAINS OF
GOODNESS

Porridge

SERVES 2 • PREPARATION TIME: NONE • COOKING TIME: 5 MINUTES • ♥ ✓ WF GF DF V

Porridge is enjoying something of a comeback after years in the highland wilderness. Not only is it low GI, which means it keeps you feeling full for longer; it also magically lowers cholesterol levels. And best of all, it's a perfect vehicle for all sorts of scrumptious toppings. We serve bucketfuls of the stuff at Leon every day and are registered addicts.

Basic Porridge

To make porridge quickly, use rolled oats – not the pinhead ones, which take ages to cook. In the restaurants we make it with whole organic milk. At home we often make it with water – it depends how creamy you are feeling.

(Oats are gluten free, but have often been milled in a mill that also processes wheat. Be sure to check if this is important to you.)

> 1 cup **rolled oats** (about 100g)
> 2 cups **water** (or **milk**, or a combination of the two)
> **salt**

1. Put the oats, water and a good pinch of salt into a pan and cook over a medium heat for 4–5 minutes, stirring as you go.
2. Serve.

Classic porridge toppers

- Cold milk with honey, a blob of jam, some dark muscovado sugar or golden syrup.
- As above, but with Jersey double cream (Sundays only).
- Banana rounds and honey (see opposite).
- Crispy streaked bacon and maple syrup (a favourite with Daddy Bear – see opposite).
- Fruity feast – an extravaganza of fresh fruit, compote, toasted nuts and seeds, and honey (see opposite).

Leon originals – favourites from the restaurant

- Valrhona chocolate flakes
- Banana, orange blossom honey and toasted seeds
- Blackberry or strawberry compote

A picture book by
WILLIAM STOBBS
The Story of the
THREE
BEARS
THE STORY OF THE THREE BEARS

Claire's Healthy Granola

MAKES 1.5KG (A GOOD AMOUNT) · PREPARATION TIME: 10 MINUTES
COOKING TIME: 1 HOUR 40 MINUTES · ♥ ✓ WF GF DF V

You will not believe how good this tastes. It is light and clustery.

500g **buckwheat flakes**	100g **coconut oil**
125g **whole almonds** (skins on)	100ml **water**
50g **ground flax seeds**	1½ teaspoons **vanilla extract**
50g **sesame seeds**	½ teaspoon **ground cinnamon**
50g **pumpkin seeds**	a grating of **fresh nutmeg**
50g **amaranth**	a pinch of **sea salt**
250ml **agave syrup**	100g **sultanas**
50ml **olive oil** (not extra virgin)	50g **desiccated coconut**

1. Heat the oven to 150°C/300°F/gas mark 2. Line 2 baking trays with baking paper.

2. Put the buckwheat flakes, whole almonds, flax seeds, sesame seeds, pumpkin seeds and amaranth into a large bowl and set aside.

3. In a saucepan, combine the agave syrup, olive oil, coconut oil and water. Place over a medium heat and whisk constantly to melt it all together without burning.

4. Remove the syrup mixture from the heat and stir in the vanilla, spices and salt. Pour the syrup over the dry ingredients and stir well to completely coat all the nuts and seeds.

5. Spread the mixture out on the baking trays and bake in the oven for approximately 1 hour.

6. Remove from the oven, toss the mixture well with a metal spatula and return to the oven. Lower the temperature to 140°C/275°F/gas mark 1 and bake for another 35–40 minutes, until the mixture is golden. Remove from the oven and allow to cool completely before stirring in the sultanas and desiccated coconut, then store in an airtight container.

TIPS

* Serve with fresh dates and low-fat natural yoghurt for a naturally sweet treat.

Hazelnut Milk

MAKES ABOUT 650ML · PREPARATION TIME: 10 MINUTES + SOAKING TIME OVERNIGHT
COOKING TIME: NONE · ♥ ✓ WF GF DF V

100g **hazelnuts,** soaked overnight or
   for 8 hours in chlorine-free water,
   drained and rinsed
seeds from ¼ of a **vanilla pod**
2 tablespoons **raw honey**
   (preferably crystallized)
600ml **water**
a tiny pinch of **sea salt**

1. In a blender, blend the soaked hazelnuts, vanilla seeds and honey
    with 200ml of the water until almost smooth.

2. Add the remaining water and blend to mix.

3. Strain through a nut milk bag, fine-mesh cheesecloth, or similar.

4. Chill and enjoy. Keeps for 6–8 days in the fridge.

Pumpkin Seed Milk

MAKES ABOUT 750ML · PREPARATION TIME: 15 MINUTES + SOAKING TIME OVERNIGHT · COOKING TIME: NONE · ♥ ✓ WF GF DF V

300g **pumpkin seeds**, soaked overnight
    or for 6–8 hours in chlorine-free water,
    drained and rinsed
40g **cashews**, soaked overnight or for
    6–8 hours in chlorine-free
    water, drained and rinsed
2 **dates,** pitted
1 tablespoon **maple syrup**
6 strokes of **grated nutmeg** (optional)
a pinch of **sea salt**
700ml **water**

1. In a blender, bend all the ingredients with 400ml of the water until almost smooth.

2. Add the remaining water and blend together.

3. Strain through a nut milk bag, fine-mesh cheesecloth, or similar.

4. Chill and enjoy. Keeps for 6–8 days in the fridge.

TIPS

* To make this milk 100% raw, omit the cashews, maple syrup and 100ml of water. Add 1 or 2 more dates.

Wonderful Yoghurt

WF GF V

1. Fill a bowl with rich natural yoghurt and cover liberally with rose petal jam (available from Middle Eastern shops).

Breakfast Bircher

MAKES 150G • PREPARATION TIME: 12 HOURS • COOKING TIME: NONE • ♥ ✓ WF GF V

150g **oats**
400ml **apple juice**

1. In a large bowl, or Tupperware box, mix the oats with the apple juice, cover and leave overnight.

TIPS

* Add flaxseeds, linseeds or any other seeds you may fancy. Soaking linseeds overnight helps to release the Omega-3s.

* Fantastic eaten with natural yoghurt and masses of chopped fruit.

Mini Knickerbocker Glory

SERVES 2 • PREPARATION TIME: 5 MINUTES • COOKING TIME: NONE • ♥ ✓ V

1 small **mango**
300g **natural yoghurt**
1–2 tablespoons **blackberry compote** or **jam**

1 tablespoon **honey**
80g **granola**

1. Peel and chop the mango into little cubes.

2. Take 2 clean medium-sized glasses and spoon a layer of yoghurt into the bottom of each one.

3. Top this with compote, followed by honey, and a further layer of yoghurt.

4. Scatter over some chopped mango, and finally top each with granola.

A Breakfasty Banana Split

SERVES 2 • PREPARATION TIME: 10 MINUTES • COOKING TIME: 5 MINUTES • WF GF V

2 **bananas**
1 **apple**
40g **nuts** – cashews, hazelnuts, macadamias
10g **butter**

2 tablespoons **natural yoghurt**
1 tablespoon **runny honey**
2 tablespoons **Breakfast Bircher** (see page 16)

1. Peel the bananas and cut them in half lengthways.

2. Core and roughly chop up the apple. Toast the nuts over a medium heat in a dry frying pan, then remove and roughly chop.

3. Heat the butter in a thick-bottomed frying pan, add the honey and cook the bananas flat side down for 3 minutes, or until golden.

4. In a clean bowl mix together the yoghurt, the bircher, the chopped apple and the toasted nuts.

5. Place the bananas on your breakfast plate (2 halves each), and top with the yoghurt and nut mixture.

WEEKEND TREATS

Jonny Jeffrey's Fluffy Eggs

SERVES 4 • PREPARATION TIME: 10 MINUTES • COOKING TIME: 8–10 MINUTES • ✓ V

This is a fantastic Sunday breakfast recipe from Kay's friend Jonny Jeffery. It's one of those classic family recipes – something his grandmother used to cook for the kids as a treat.

4 **free-range eggs**
4 slices of **bread**
small handful of finely grated **cheese** –
    Cheddar, Parmesan, Emmental,
    whichever you prefer
salt and **freshly ground black pepper**

1. Heat the oven to 190°C/375°F/gas mark 5.

2. Separate the eggs, keeping the yolks whole, and whisk the egg whites into stiff peaks.

3. Lightly toast the bread, then put the slices on a baking tray. Spread three-quarters of the egg white on to the semi-toasted bread.

4. Make a small well in the egg white on each slice of bread, and pop in a yolk – one yolk per slice. Season each yolk with salt and pepper, then cover with the remaining egg white, making sure the yolk is sealed in.

5. Sprinkle a teaspoon of grated cheese over each, then bake in the oven for 8–10 minutes, or until the top is nicely golden. This should give you a nice, runny yolk. If you prefer a firmer yolk, give it a little longer. Serve at once.

TIPS

When we were kids, we used to call our granny More Granny because we were always saying, 'Please can we have some more, Granny.' Her fluffy eggs were always one of my favourites.

JONNY

* When Jonny cooked this for us, he served it with some delicious pan-fried chorizo, but you could try it with bacon, smoked salmon, black pudding or even some sautéed mushrooms.

* Why not, as Jonny suggests, use duck eggs instead. Then you can call it Fluffy Ducks.

* The surface area of your slice of toast is important. The smaller the slice, the higher you must pile your egg whites, which slightly affects the cooking time. We recommend slices from a large white or brown loaf.

Perfect Scrambled Eggs

SERVES 2 • PREPARATION TIME: 5 MINUTES • COOKING TIME: 5–10 MINUTES • ✓ WF GF V

In the short story *007 in New York*, Ian Fleming gives one of the definitive recipes for scrambled eggs with cream and finely chopped *fines herbes*. But let's save the full Bond for the weekend: for an everyday breakfast, we won't be quite so indulgent.

5 **free-range eggs**
a dash of **milk**
a good pinch of chopped **fresh parsley,**
    or **basil**, or **coriander**, or **thyme** (optional)
1 tablespoon **butter**
salt and **freshly ground black pepper**

1. Crack the eggs into a bowl, add the milk, salt and pepper (and the pinch of chopped herbs, if you're using them), and beat them all together with a fork.

2. In a heavy-based pan, melt the butter over a medium heat until it starts to foam. Pour in the eggs, and start stirring at once with a fork or a wooden spoon. Keep stirring constantly as the eggs start to come together.

3. The question now is: how runny do you like them? As the eggs begin to come together, start turning down the heat – they'll keep cooking in the residual heat. Keep stirring until you've got them just how you like them, and serve out on to plates at once. Bear in mind, the eggs at the bottom of the pan will be firmer than the eggs you serve first – just in case some people prefer them one way or the other.

4. Garnish with an extra grind of black pepper and tuck in.

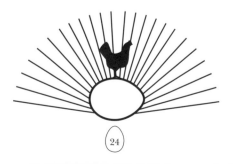

Perfect Poached Eggs

SERVES 4 • PREPARATION TIME: 10 MINUTES • COOKING TIME: 1.5 MINUTES • ✓ WF GF DF V

Kay never used to cook a lot of poached eggs until chef Bryn Williams, of Odette's in Primrose Hill, London, told her his infallible method. As he says, if you have to make fifty of the darned things a day, you want something foolproof. This is it.

4 **free-range eggs**
1 teaspoon **salt**
1 tablespoon **white wine vinegar**
1 bowl of **iced water** – if you're
   not serving them at once

1. Crack the eggs into 4 individual ramekins or small dishes.

2. Fill the deepest saucepan you can find with water, add the salt and vinegar, and bring to a rolling boil. One by one, add the eggs. They will sink to the bottom of the pan, and as they do, you will see the white coming up and around the yolk. After about a minute, the eggs will start to rise up through the water. At this point, if you're making them ahead of time, scoop the eggs out with a slotted spoon and plunge them immediately into the bowl of iced water to stop them cooking. When they're cold, remove them from the water and set aside until you need them. If you're serving them now, cook them for a further 30 seconds to 1 minute in the boiling water for a firm white and a good runny yolk.

3. To reheat, bring a pan of clean water to the boil, add the cooled eggs and heat through for about 30 seconds to 1 minute.

TIPS

* **Perfect Soft Boiled Eggs**
Ease an egg into salted boiling water and cook for 3 minutes & 33 seconds

Posh Poached Eggs in a Cup

WITH CHORIZO & TRUFFLED CHEESE

SERVES 4 • PREPARATION TIME: 5 MINUTES • COOKING TIME: 10–15 MINUTES

On our breakfast menu at Leon, we have what we call Egg Cups. We poach eggs in a small pot and add a few things – the don't-you-ever-take-it-off-the-menu combination is truffle, Gruyère and sliced chorizo. No chorizo to hand? It also works well with shredded ham or bacon. And once you've tried it, it'll never come off your breakfast menu either.

4–8 **free-range eggs**
100g **chorizo**, thinly sliced
1 tablespoon **white vinegar**,
   for poaching
salt and **freshly ground**
   black pepper

For the cheese sauce:
25g **unsalted butter**
25g **gram flour**
350ml **milk**
120g **Gruyère cheese**, grated
½ teaspoon **truffle oil**

1. First make the sauce: melt the butter in a saucepan over a medium heat. Add the gram flour and whisk the two together until smooth and all the flour is incorporated in the butter and cooks out – about 2 minutes.

2. Add the milk a little at a time, whisking as you go, until you have a smooth lump-free sauce. Keep whisking until it thickens slightly, enough to coat the back of a spoon. Add the grated cheese and the truffle oil and whisk well until everything is combined and glossy, then season with salt and pepper. Set aside and keep warm.

3. In a non-stick pan, heat the olive oil over a medium heat and fry the chorizo until the slices are cooked through and crisp. Remove the chorizo from the pan and drain on kitchen paper.

4. Poach the eggs (one or two each, depending on how hungry everyone is) following the method on page 25.

5. Grind some pepper and a little sea salt on top of each egg, then pop them into their cups (I use a small teacup or similar sort of thing). Sprinkle a quarter of the chorizo on top of each egg, then pour on a quarter of the cheese sauce and grind a little more pepper on top.

6. Nummy nummy, as John's daughter Natasha used to say.

Omelette Baveuse

THE WORLD'S GREATEST OMELETTE

PREPARATION TIME: 2 MINUTES • COOKING TIME: 2–3 MINUTES • ✓ WF GF V

Discovering an omelette 'baveuse' is a game-changing moment in life. We were taught how to make them by our French friend Pierre. Many people leave the centre of the omelette a little moist or tacky like this, but there is a particular quality that can only come from cooking them at a low heat.

2 **free-range eggs** per person
1 tablespoon grated **Cheddar cheese** per person
1 heaped spoonful of **crème fraîche** per person
a dash of **vegetable oil**
sea salt and **freshly ground black pepper**

1. Put the eggs, cheese, seasoning and crème fraîche into a bowl. Whip them up a little with a fork so that they are well mixed.

2. Get a non-stick pan reasonably hot and heat a dash of vegetable oil.

3. Pour in the egg mixture and tilt the pan so that it spreads around the base. With a wooden spatula, circle the edge of the pan and ensure that the edges remain loose. After 15 seconds reduce the heat to low.

4. When the top has a moist, tacky texture (see opposite), use the spatula to fold one side of the omelette over on to itself and slide it on to a plate. The omelette should be just coloured on the underside, and still slightly runny inside.

5. Eat immediately.

IPS

* If you want to make the omelette a little healthier you can leave out the cheese and crème fraîche (or replace the crème fraîche with a little whole milk).

* Thirty seconds into cooking you can add a filling. We particularly like:
  Healthy: Tomato and turmeric. Heat a little oil in a very hot pan. Roughly chop a tomato (1 per person) and add it to the smoking oil. Toss vigorously – some of the oil may well flare up, so don't

do this in flammable pyjamas. Add a generous pinch of turmeric and season well. The tomatoes should still have shape but will be a bit saucy.
Classic & Classy: Add fromage frais, smoked salmon and chives.
Cheesy: Add 50g more grated cheese per person, with chopped chives and parsley.
Mushroomy: Put Ultimate Mushrooms on Toast (page 51) inside the omelette.
Hammy: Prosciutto, crispy bacon or any other finely chopped cured meat.

Eggy Bread

2 tablespoons **unsalted butter**, plus extra to serve
5 **free-range eggs**
400ml **whole milk**
1 tablespoon **pure vanilla extract**
75g **caster sugar**
½ teaspoon **ground cinnamon**
8–12 slices of good **stale bread**
icing sugar, for dusting the top
maple syrup, to serve

1. Heat a large heavy frying pan and drop in a little of the butter.

2. In a large shallow bowl, whisk together the eggs, milk, vanilla, sugar and cinnamon.

3. Place a couple of slices of bread in the eggy mixture and dunk it down, piercing the slices with tiny holes. Once the bread seems saturated, flip the slices over.

4. The pan should now be ready and the butter sizzling.

5. Carefully lift the slices of bread from the eggy mixture and place in the frying pan.

6. Brown the bread well on both sides, meanwhile repeating the dunking process with the remaining slices of bread.

7. Place on a plate, set in a warm place and butter the slices.

8. Dust the finished slices of buttered eggy bread with icing sugar and serve with maple syrup.

TIPS

* You can use all types of white crusty bread, as well as sourdough if you fancy it.
* Be sure to soak the bread with lots of eggy mixture. And don't be shy with the butter in the pan. You want a moist, custard-like middle and a crisp exterior.
* Serve with fresh berries in the summer.
* Try slices of ripe bananas with a pinch of cinnamon.
* Add orange or lemon zest to the eggy mixture for a nice bright flavour.

Deconstructed Huevos Rancheros

WITH A FRESH PEPPER & CHILLI SALSA

SERVES 4 · PREPARATION TIME: 15 MINUTES · COOKING TIME: 10 MINUTES · ♥ ✓ WF GF DF V

This Mexican breakfast dish is usually made with a fried egg, served on fried corn tortillas with refried beans and a cooked tomato and onion salsa on the side. All we've done here is pulled back on the oil by poaching the eggs, plumped for a fresh salsa, and served some simple black beans and steamed corn tortillas on the side making it lighter.

For the pepper & chilli salsa:
1 **Romano pepper**, deseeded
1 **green Serrano chilli,** deseeded
2 **tomatoes**, deseeded
1 **shallot**
2–3 cloves of **garlic**
a few leaves of **fresh basil**
a squeeze of **lime juice**
a dash of **olive oil**
salt and **freshly ground
   black pepper**

1 x 400g tin of **black beans**
1 teaspoon **dried oregano**
4–8 **corn tortillas**
4 **free-range eggs**
salt and **freshly ground
   black pepper**

1. First make the salsa: finely chop the pepper, chilli, tomatoes, shallot and garlic, and mix them together in a bowl. Rip in the basil leaves, add the lime juice and olive oil, and season with salt and pepper. Stir together, taste for seasoning, then set aside.

2. Now empty the black beans into a pan – don't strain them, you want their liquid. Gently heat them, adding the oregano and a pinch of salt and pepper. Set aside to keep warm.

3. Wrap the corn tortillas in a clean tea towel and steam over boiling water (preferably in a tiered steamer) until they are piping hot – just takes a couple of minutes. Set aside to keep warm.

4. Finally, poach the eggs (see page 25). To serve, lay 1 or 2 warm corn tortillas on each plate and top with the eggs, beans and salsa.

TIPS

* Make sure to use pure corn tortillas. We've found that a lot of the commercial tortillas available have wheat in them. This is also delicious with some sliced avocado or guacamole on the side.

The Grill Up with Easy Poached Eggs

SERVES 2 • PREPARATION TIME: NONE • COOKING TIME: 20 MINUTES • ✓DF

Like many good things in life, this is all about timing.

2 **tomatoes**
2 large or 4 small **flat, field** or
  Portobello mushrooms
olive oil
2 **free-range eggs**
4 rashers of your favourite **bacon**

2 fat or 4 thin **pork sausages**
1 slice of **bread** per person
  (optional)
sea salt and **freshly ground
  black pepper**

1. Turn your grill on fairly high. Tear off a sheet of foil and put it shiny side down on a wide baking sheet. Cut your tomatoes and put them at one end in a row, followed by a neat row of whole mushrooms. Drizzle with a little olive oil and season well. Place the sausages on the tray as well. Pop the tray under the grill – on the highest shelf.

2. Set up 2 teacups and tear off a piece of clingfilm for each one. Line the teacups and crack an egg into each. (If you are a confident egg poacher with super-fresh eggs, just do it your normal way at the end.)

3. Put the bacon on the grilling tray and return it to the grill. Boil a kettle.

4. Bring up the edges of the clingfilm to a tight twist, leaving a little airspace next to the egg.

5. Fill a small saucepan two-thirds full with boiling water, and put the pan on to boil.

6. Turn the sausages and bacon and pop back under the grill for a further 5 minutes.

7. If you like to have toast, get your bread under the grill or in the toaster.

8. Gently drop your egg parcels into the boiling water in the pan, turn the heat down to a simmer and set your timer for 4 minutes for soft eggs or 5 for hard.

9. Assemble your brekkie on 2 plates. The eggs will be fine out of the water, in their clingfilm, for a minute or two.

Saturday Pancakes

SERVES 4 · PREPARATION TIME: 15 MINUTES · COOKING TIME: 15 MINUTES · ♥ WF

For a luxurious – but wheat-free – start to Saturday morning.

3 **free-range eggs**
125g **buckwheat flour**
1 large teaspoon **honey**
a large pinch of **baking powder**
140ml organic **milk**
sea salt

1. Separate the eggs. Place the yolks in a large bowl and add the buckwheat flour.

2. Add the honey, baking powder and a pinch of salt and mix thoroughly. Slowly add the milk to make a smooth batter. You can do all this the night before.

3. In a separate bowl, whisk the egg whites to firm peaks and fold gently into the yolk mixture.

4. Heat a non-stick pan, gently drop in spoonfuls of the mixture, and cook for 2–3 minutes on each side.

TIPS

You can devise all sorts of toppings for your pancakes, but here are three of our favourites:

- **Luxury:** Caramelized apple and cream. Foam a blob of butter in a pan, toss in diced apples (1 apple per person), a sprinkling of cinnamon and a little sugar and fry till brown. Take off the heat and stir in some double cream at the end.

- **Fruity:** Blueberries, sliced banana and agave syrup.

- **John's Chocolate Pancakes:** John will eat chocolate with almost anything. This makes a surprisingly good breakfast. Banana, grated dark chocolate (70 per cent cocoa solids) and agave syrup.

Mixed Fruit

WITH GREEK YOGHURT & BROWN MOLASSES SUGAR

SERVES 4 • PREPARATION TIME: 10 MINUTES • COOKING TIME: NONE • WF GF V

A straightforward breakfast treat that can be made in advance.

> 1 large ripe **mango**
> 1 **kiwi fruit**
> 100g **blueberries** or **blackberries**
> 100g **strawberries**
> 1 **passion fruit**
> 500g tub of **Greek yoghurt**
> 3–4 heaped tablespoons
>   **dark brown molasses sugar**

1. Peel and chop the mango and kiwi into cubes and place in a large mixing bowl.

2. Add the berries and the passion fruit seeds and mix well.

3. Chose an attractive serving bowl, or individual bowls if you want, and spoon in the chopped fruit.

4. Top generously with the Greek yoghurt, so that it covers all the fruit in a thick layer.

5. Scatter over the molasses sugar – it will start to soak into the yoghurt, but you will notice that some remains in clumps and forms delicious toffee-like blobs.

TIPS

* Add more sugar if you like it swimming in the melted molasses.

* If you are making this in advance, you can either add the sugar just before serving, or add it earlier, let it soak into the yoghurt and add extra at the last minute.

* Use any combination of fruit. Berries and stoned fruits work the best.

BREADS
&
BAKES

Gluten-free Bread

MAKES I LOAF • PREPARATION TIME: 20 MINUTES + I HOUR RISING TIME
COOKING TIME: 55 MINUTES • ♥ WF GF V

The gluten in a loaf gives it that chewy interior and tender crumb. Take the gluten out and you get something a little denser of crumb and a bit more cake-like. In its own right, however, it is very satisfying.

500g **gluten-free brown bread flour**
½ teaspoon **sea salt**
2 x 7g sachets **dried quick yeast**
2 tablespoons **honey**
325ml **milk**
1 tablespoon **cider vinegar**
2 tablespoons **olive oil**
2 **free-range eggs**
poppy seeds, for sprinkling

1. Grease a 450g/1lb loaf tin.

2. Combine the flour, salt and yeast and set aside.

3. Warm the honey and milk slightly and remove from the heat. Add the vinegar and oil and whisk in the eggs.

4. Add the wet ingredients to the dry ingredients and bring together to form a dough. Then shape the dough into a log. Place it in your prepared tin, sprinkle with water and then scatter poppy seeds over the top, to cover. Put the dough in a warm place and leave to rise for 1 hour.

5. Heat the oven to 200°C/400°F/gas mark 6 and bake for 45–55 minutes.

6. Leave to cool in the tin for 5 minutes before turning out on to a wire rack to cool completely.

TIPS

* Try adding some seeds to the dough to vary the texture and flavour of this loaf. It is always a good idea to soak the seeds overnight before adding them to the bread mixture, because soaking the seeds increases the amount of vitamins your body can absorb from them.

Raw Nut & Seed Butters

One of the best things to spread on your bread first thing in the morning is a homemade nut butter. They are both indulgent and fantastically good for you.

1. Choose good-quality, very fresh raw walnuts, almonds, pumpkin seeds, hazelnuts, cashews or sunflower seeds.

2. If you like, you can soak or sprout the nuts or seeds first. If you do this, make sure you dry them well before processing them.

3. Process the nuts or seeds in a food processor for several minutes to extract all the oil. As the nuts and seeds are whizzing round, you can drizzle in a little raw honey or water to help turn it into an emulsified butter.

4. Store in the fridge.

OPPOSITE FROM TOP: HAZELNUT BUTTER; PUMPKIN SEED BUTTER; CASHEW NUT BUTTER; ALMOND BUTTER.

Flour Station Rye Bread

MAKES I LOAF · PREPARATION TIME: I HOUR + I HOUR RESTING AND PROVING TIME
COOKING TIME: 55 MINUTES · ♥ ✓ WF D F V

This bread is baked for us by the magnificent bakers at London's Flour Station, who add baked potatoes to the dough to keep it moist. It has a lovely springy texture, with nutty sunflower seeds adding bite.

25g **rye starter** (50% water/50% rye flour)
100g **baking potatoes**
1½ teaspoons **water**
100g **rye flour**, plus extra for dusting

10g **dried yeast**
2 teaspoons **salt**
100g s**unflower seeds**
2 tablespoons **molasses** or **black treacle**

1. First make your rye starter by weighing 100g or organic dark rye flour and 100g of warm water and stirring them together in a jar with a sealed lid – a kilner jar is ideal. Leave the jar in a prominent and warm place in your kitchen with the lid sealed. Each day for a week repeat the feeding process. Put 100g of the starter in a bowl (discarding the surplus or using it to flavour cakes, buns, pancakes and pizza dough), add 100g of water and 100g of flour and stir vigorously to remove all floury lumps with a clean finger or a fork. Return it to the jar. After about 5 days you'll notice bubbles in the dough – meaning that it's ready to be used. From now on, you can keep it in the fridge, removing it a couple of days before use to feed it back into full bubbly liveliness.

2. Bake the potatoes and allow them to cool, then peel them.

3. Put all the ingredients into a mixing bowl (avoiding direct contact between the fresh yeast and the salt).

4. In a free-standing mixer with a dough hook, mix on a slow speed until everything is blended, or mix by hand. The dough will be very wet and sticky, but after a while the colour will change slightly from brown to a lighter, more yellow colour.

5. Cover the bowl with a damp cloth and leave the dough to rest for approximately 3 hours, or until the dough is 'active' or bubbling.

6. Butter a 900g/2lb loaf tin and dust it with rye flour.

7. Dust the table with rye flour and turn out the dough. Shape and place in the prepared loaf tin. Press down lightly and dust the top with rye flour.

8. Leave in a warm, draught-free place to 'prove' (or rise), until you see cracks appearing on the surface of the dough. It should increase in size by approximately 50%.

9. Heat the oven to 220°C/425°F/gas mark 7. Dust the dough with rye flour again and bake in the oven for 55 minutes, or until the loaf has a rich dark crust.

TIPS

* This bread actually improves with age and is best enjoyed the day after baking. It will stay fresh for at least a week, as the potatoes attract moisture and therefore keep the bread moist for longer.

* Toast thin slices of this bread and top with butter or coconut oil and a nut butter (see page 45).

Topped Rye Bread

Of all the quick breakfasts, these are the quickest. Rye bread freezes well and toasts directly from frozen. It is wheat, and often yeast, free. Most importantly, the modern rye breads no longer taste of Ukrainian footwear. They are soft and sweet and remarkably moreish.

What follows are ideas rather than recipes – we hope they will spark you into making some rye creations of your own.

New York Breakfast WF

The classic rye breakfast. Toast the rye. Smear on cream cheese. Top with smoked salmon, cucumber rings, chopped ripe tomatoes and finely sliced red onion. Squeeze over some lemon juice and sprinkle with chopped chives.

Cream Cheese & Blackcurrant Jam WF V

Think yoghurt and jam, but on an open sandwich.

Peanut Butter & White Grapes ♥ WF DF V

This is the healthy version of peanut butter and jello. Slice the grapes in half and either plonk them loosely on the peanut butter or arrange them in military rows for that classic 70s look.

Other rye toppers we love

- **The Continental:** Like the New York breakfast, but substitute a good ham for the smoked salmon.

- **The Fruit & Nut:** Any other combination of fruit and peanut butter. Fine slices of apple are particularly good.

- **Hot Berries:** Heat honey, ground cinnamon and berries in a pan until the berries begin to lose their edges. Pop on to the rye and top with a blob of yoghurt.

- **The Wimbledon:** Strawberries and banana tossed in a little thick yoghurt, with a touch of honey drizzled on top.

- **Honey & Banana Slices:** Spread the honey on the rye and arrange the banana slices geometrically, just because it looks pretty.

- **The Full English:** Sliced tomatoes (on the bottom), scrambled egg and a crispy slice of thin streaky bacon.

- **The Veggie English:** Sliced tomatoes, topped with mushrooms that have been quick-fried in super-hot olive oil.

- **The Reichstag:** Wholegrain mustard on the bottom, then sliced tomatoes, ham and finely sliced dill pickles. For extremists only.

Ultimate Mushrooms on Toast

A chef friend of ours once said that he believed the common button mushroom would be an expensive delicacy if it was rare. The way that it colours and deepens in flavour as it cooks is a wonder. Don't feel you need fancy mushrooms to make the ultimate mushrooms on toast.

1. A good bread, toasted.

2. Butter, spread on the toast.

3. A good knob of butter and a trickle of vegetable oil in a hot pan. The butter should foam.

4. A generous handful of sliced button mushrooms thrown into the pan with a tablespoon of finely sliced onion. Don't move them around too much. Toss every 30 seconds or so, but give them time to go golden. Season with salt and pepper.

5. Finely chopped garlic and fresh parsley thrown in for the last 30 seconds.

6. A squeeze of lemon juice and on to the toast.

Variations on a theme

*   **Luxury:** Instead of lemon juice add a splash of white wine at the end. When this has bubbled off, add a tablespoon of double cream and bubble for 20 seconds before offloading on to the toast.

*   **Meaty:** Before you cook the mushrooms, fry some prosciutto in the pan until it goes crispy. Stick it on top like a shark's fin.

*   **Toast on Mushrooms on Toast:** This was an accident we discovered while photographing the pictures for this book. Nothing in the world tastes better. Fry some breadcrumbs with garlic and seasoning until they are crispy. Make the Ultimate Mushrooms on Toast. Sprinkle the garlic breadcrumbs on top for extra crunch.

Ralph's Mango Lassi

SERVES 2 • PREPARATION TIME: 15–20 MINUTES • COOKING TIME: NONE • ♥ WF GF V

A lovely cooling drink, especially in hot weather, this is also a great and fruity way to start the day.

> 300ml **live yoghurt** (low-fat if preferred), chilled
> 4 ripe chilled **mangoes**, peeled, stoned and chopped
> 30ml **clear honey**
> 15ml **lime juice**
> 2 cups of **ice cubes**
> sprigs of **fresh mint**, to garnish

1. Combine the yoghurt, mangoes, honey, lime juice in a blender. Add ice and blend for 15 seconds, until smooth.

2. Serve garnished with sprigs of mint.

TIPS

* You can use buttermilk in place of the yoghurt if you prefer.

* If you can't find decent ripe mangoes, you can buy unsweetened mango pulp in cans at most large supermarkets.

* For a more savoury version, leave out the honey and add a teaspoon of salt and a couple of pinches of ground cardamom.

RALPH, BANGKOK, 1988

Lovely Ralph Monthienvichienchai is literally MADD about mangoes, so much so that he opened a dessert bar of the same name in London. If you need to know anything about mangoes, he's your guy. Thanks to him for this delicious recipe.

Hattie's Super-Healthy Almond Smoothie

SERVES 2 • PREPARATION TIME: 5 MINUTES • COOKING TIME: NONE • ♥ WF DF GF V

And for those who are looking for something dairy free …

  1 **kiwi fruit**
  1 **banana**
  2 large handfuls of **berries** – whatever is in season
  8 **almonds**, skins on
  2 heaped tablespoons **oats**
  1 tablespoon **pumpkin seeds**
  1 tablespoon **sunflower seeds**
  250ml **rice milk**, **almond milk** or **soya milk**

1. Peel the kiwis and the banana. Wash the berries.
2. Put all the ingredients into a smoothie machine or a blender and blitz together until smooth.

Tiger's Milk

SERVES 1 • PREPARATION TIME: 3 MINUTES • COOKING TIME: 2–3 MINUTES • WF GF V

Tiger, Tiger, burning bright … No, no — not THAT kind of tiger! You think we're mad enough to try to milk one? No, this was the only way anyone could get the small Kay to drink milk. The tale went that it was 'tiger's milk' because it was stripy … Kay can't for the life of her believe that she fell for that one! The honey 'stripes' disappear after about three seconds, so she must have been an extraordinarily gullible child!

1 mug of **milk**
1 small **stick of cinnamon**
1 tablespoon **honey**
an extra pinch of **ground cinnamon** (optional)

1. Heat the milk in a pan until it's just warm – you don't want it too hot. Then use an immersion blender to froth the milk. This guarantees you will get stripes.

2. Pop the cinnamon stick into the mug and pour the warmed milk over it. Now – watch for it – drizzle the spoonful of honey into the milk, from a height, in concentric circles. See those stripes? Stir it in with the cinnamon stick and add an extra pinch of cinnamon, if you like.

LUNE & KAY, 1965

Lune was a huge part of our family, and was my nanny when I was growing up. She was also the manufacturer of this particular tall tale. We adored each other. Except for when she tried to comb the tangles out of my perpetually wayward hair. Then I wasn't so keen.

KAY

CONVERSION CHART FOR COMMON MEASURE

LIQUIDS

15 ml	$1/2$ fl oz
25 ml	1 fl oz
50 ml	2 fl oz
75 ml	3 fl oz
100ml	$3 1/2$ fl oz
125 ml	4 fl oz
150 ml	$1/4$ pint
175 ml	6 fl oz
200 ml	7 fl oz
250 ml	8 fl oz
275 ml	9 fl oz
300 ml	$1/2$ pint
325 ml	11 fl oz
350 ml	12 fl oz
375 ml	13 fl oz
400 ml	14 fl oz
450 ml	$3/4$ pint
475 ml	16 fl oz
500 ml	17 fl oz
575 ml	18 fl oz
600 ml	1 pint
750 ml	$1 1/4$ pints
900 ml	$1 1/2$ pints
1 litre	$1 3/4$ pints
1.2 litres	2 pints
1.5 litres	$2 1/2$ pints
1.8 litres	3 pints
2 litres	$3 1/2$ pints
2.5 litres	4 pints
3.6 litres	6 pints

WEIGHTS

5 g	$1/4$ oz
15 g	$1/2$ oz
20 g	$3/4$ oz
25 g	1 oz
50 g	2 oz
75 g	3 oz
125 g	4 oz
150 g	5 oz
175 g	6 oz
200 g	7 oz
250 g	8 oz
275 g	9 oz
300 g	10 oz
325 g	11 oz
375 g	12 oz
400 g	13 oz
425 g	14 oz
475 g	15 oz
500 g	1 lb
625 g	$1 1/4$ lb
750 g	$1 1/2$ lb
875 g	$1 3/4$ lb
1 kg	2 lb
1.25 kg	$2 1/2$ lb
1.5 kg	3 lb
1.75 kg	$3 1/2$ lb
2 kg	4 lb

OVEN TEMPERATURES

110°C	(225°F)	Gas Mark $1/4$
120°C	(250°F)	Gas Mark $1/2$
140°C	(275°F)	Gas Mark 1
150°C	(300°F)	Gas Mark 2
160°C	(325°F)	Gas Mark 3
180°C	(350°F)	Gas Mark 4
190°C	(375°F)	Gas Mark 5
200°C	(400°F)	Gas Mark 6
220°C	(425°F)	Gas Mark 7
230°C	(450°F)	Gas Mark 8

MEASUREMENTS

5 mm	$1/4$ inch
1 cm	$1/2$ inch
1.5 cm	$3/4$ inch
2.5 cm	1 inch
5 cm	2 inches
7 cm	3 inches
10 cm	4 inches
12 cm	5 inches
15 cm	6 inches
18 cm	7 inches
20 cm	8 inches
23 cm	9 inches
25 cm	10 inches
28 cm	11 inches
30 cm	12 inches
33 cm	13 inches

Working with different types of oven

All the recipes in this book have been tested in an oven without a fan. If you are using a fan-assisted oven, lower the temperature given in the recipe by 20°C. Modern fan-assisted ovens are very efficient at circulating heat evenly around the oven, so there's also no need to worry about positioning.

Regardless of what type of oven you use you will find that it has its idiosyncrasies, so don't stick slavishly to any baking recipes. Make sure you understand how your oven behaves and adjust accordingly.

Key to Symbols/Nutritional Info

♥	LOW SATURATED FATS
✓	LOW GLYCEMIC (GI) LOAD
WF	WHEAT FREE
GF	GLUTEN FREE
DF	DAIRY FREE
V	VEGETARIAN
ⓤ	INDULGENCE
TIPS	COOKING TIPS, EXTRA INFORMATION AND ALTERNATIVE IDEAS.

Index

An Hachette UK Company
www.hachette.co.uk

First published in Great Britain in 2013 by Conran Octopus Limited,
a division of Octopus Publishing Group Ltd,
Carmelite House, 50 Victoria Embankment, London EC4Y 0DZ
www.octopusbooks.co.uk

This book includes a selection of previously published recipes taken from the following titles:
Leon Naturally Fast Food; Leon Baking & Puddings; Leon Family & Friends.

ISBN 978 1 84091 624 9

A CIP catalogue record for this book is available from the British Library.

Printed and bound in China

10 9 8 7 6 5 4

Publisher: Alison Starling
Senior Editor: Sybella Stephens
Assistant Editor: Stephanie Milner
Art Director: Jonathan Christie
Art Direction, Design & Illustrations: Anita Mangan
Design Assistant: Abigail Read
Photography: Georgia Glynn Smith
Production Manager: Katherine Hockley

A note from the authors…
Medium eggs should be used unless otherwise stated.
We have endeavoured to be as accurate as possible in all the preparation and cooking times listing
in the recipes in this book. However they are an estimate based on our own timings during recipe
testing, and should be taken as a guide only, not as the literal truth. We have also tried to source all
our food facts carefully, but we are not scientists. So our food facts and nutrition advice are not
absolute. If you feel you require consultation with a nutritionist, consult your GP for a recommendation.